HEATHCLIFF
ON VACATION

The funniest feline in America delights millions
of fans every day as he appears in over 500 news-
papers. You'll have a laugh a minute as Heathcliff
tangles with the milkman, the mailman, the veteri-
narian and just about everyone else he runs into.
If you're looking for some fun, look no further.
Heathcliff is here.

HEATHCLIFF®
ON VACATION

by
Geo Gately

C

CHARTER BOOKS, NEW YORK

Cartoons previously published in
the Tempo/Charter trade paperback
Heathcliff Feast

HEATHCLIFF ON VACATION

A Charter Book / published by arrangement with
McNaught Syndicate, Inc.

PRINTING HISTORY
Special Charter Book Club edition / March 1986

Charter Books are published by The Berkley Publishing Group,
200 Madison Avenue, New York, New York 10016.
PRINTED IN THE UNITED STATES OF AMERICA

"HE'S IN GREAT SHAPE, BUT I NEED A DOCTOR!"

"TIMB . . . . ER!"

"FANCY MEETING YOU HERE!"

"WELL, HOW WOULD **YOU** LIKE TO BE SAT ON?"

"THAT'S THE THIRD TIME THIS WEEK THAT CAT HAS DISRUPTED OUR CLASSROOM!"

"I DON'T KNOW...I THINK IT'S A TOSS-UP WHICH ONE IS WORSE."

"IT'S HIS HOT LINE TO THE DAIRY FARM."

"OH-OH...."

"HE BROKE UP THE BRIDGE CLUB AGAIN."

© 1974
McNaught Synd., Inc.

5-27

"HEATHCLIFF LOVES TO SHAKE UP COLONEL BOOMER."

"NOW PROMISE MAMA YOU WON'T DO TO *THIS* MAN WHAT YOU DID TO THE *LAST* ONE."

"THAT'S WHAT YOU GET FOR RIFLING
THE BRANDIED PEACHES."

"THERE YOU GO, PLAYING FAVORITES AGAIN!"

"TOO MUCH HOWLING LAST NIGHT?"

"LOOK INTO MY EYES..."

"MEOW.... MEOW.... MEOW...."

"I WONDER IF HEATHCLIFF HAS NOTICED
OUR NEW NEIGHBOR'S FEMALE CAT YET?"

"SIX SLIPPERS AND THREE BOOTS...
HE MUST HAVE MADE QUITE A RACKET
LAST NIGHT!"

"THAT WILL BE $18.50 FOR YOUR SWEATER AND $16.98 FOR *HIS*!"

"NO, BUT I'LL KEEP AN EYE OPEN."

"WELL, SO MUCH FOR OUR NEIGHBOR'S
NEW WATCH-DOG."

"JUST DROP THEM IN HIS MOUTH...
IT'S HIS BIRTHDAY."

"I CAN'T UNDERSTAND IT...
BESSIE HARDLY GAVE ANY MILK TODAY."

"TWO BANANA SPLITS...ONE WITH
WALNUTS AND ONE WITH ANCHOVIES."

"WHAT MADE YOU THINK HIS BITE
NEEDED CORRECTING?!"

"SUP........PER!"

"NEXT TIME, GET HIS NAILS CLIPPED!"

"THERE'S A SIGHT YOU DON'T SEE
VERY OFTEN."

11-17

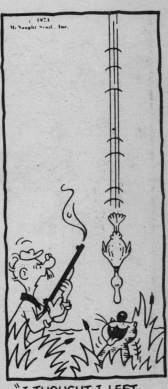

"I THOUGHT I LEFT YOU HOME!"

"ABOUT THAT FROZEN PIZZA.."

"ARE THEY ALL FLYING SOUTH FOR
THE WINTER, GRANDPA?"

"NOT WILLINGLY."

"GRANDMA, WAIT'LL I SHOW YOU
WHAT HEATHCLIFF BROUGHT HOME,
ONCE IT STOPS WRIGGLING."

"HEATHCLIFF!"

"IT'S THAT PESTY CAT AGAIN!"

"GET IN THERE, HEATHCLIFF
AND BITE THE FULLBACK!"

"THERE ARE A LOT OF CAT FIGHTS IN THIS
NEIGHBORHOOD... MOSTLY BETWEEN
ME AND HEATHCLIFF!"

"I THINK HE'S BEEN HITTING THE CATNIP
AGAIN."

"HERE COMES THE PUNCH, FOLKS!"

"DUE TO CIRCUMSTANCES BEYOND OUR CONTROL..."

"HELP!"

"THEN AGAIN, IN SOME WAYS, THEY'RE
VERY MUCH ALIKE."

"WE THINK HEATHCLIFF IS PART PERSIAN AND PART SIAMESE."

"I'D SAY PART TIGER AND PART ALLEY."

"NOW, HOW DID HE GET OUT OF
HIS CARRIAGE?"

"WE'RE DOWN HERE, GRANDMA...
ENTERTAINING MRS. FINCHLEY."

"HEATHCLIFF CAUGHT *THAT* ONE."

"HEATHCLIFF NEVER COULD RESIST TWEED."

"HEAVY DATE TONIGHT?"

"HOW ABOUT . . .

. . . THAT ! "

"I TRIED PUTTING HEATHCLIFF
ON A DIET TODAY."

"WHATEVER YOU DO, DON'T BRING UP
THE SUBJECT OF CATS."

"THE SITTER LEFT SHORTLY AFTER YOU DID."

"...AND IT'S A VERY PEACEFUL NEIGHBORHOOD..."

"...WITH *ONE* EXCEPTION..."

"NEVER MIND THE DISGUISE!...
I KNOW IT'S YOU!!"

"I CAN'T UNDERSTAND IT... I'VE BEEN DRUMMED OUT OF THE SOCIETY OF BIRD WATCHERS!"

"AND NOW BACK TO OUR MOVIE ...
'CURSE OF THE CAT PEOPLE'..."

"HE ATE MY STETHOSCOPE!"

"COME ON, FOLKS...DINNER'S ON THE TABLE."

"HEATHCLIFF COLLECTS THEM."

"HELP!"

"FOUR AND TWENTY BLACKBIRDS, BAKED IN A PIE..."

"HE SINGS HERE EVERY NIGHT."

"HOW MANY TIMES MUST I TELL YOU,
THEY'RE NOT MOUSE HOLES!"

"OH, HE DOESN'T READ THEM...HE CHEWS THEM."

"I'M WARNING YOU FOR THE LAST TIME...SCAT!"

"HE CERTAINLY HAS MADE A NAME
FOR HIMSELF IN THIS TOWN."

© 1974
McNaught Synd., Inc.

"OH, HELLO, MACTAVISH....HMMMM ?...
HEATHCLIFF STOLE *WHAT* FROM YOUR SCOTTY?"

"HE DOES THAT EVERYTIME THE PRICE GOES UP!"

© 1974
McNaught
Syndicate, Inc 3-8

"HE KNOWS VERY WELL WHAT HAT!"

"FOR SOME UNKNOWN REASON, HE TOOK
A DISLIKE TO THE CIRCUS STRONG MAN."

"THIS CAR IS GETTING A TERRIBLE SQUEAK IN IT!"

"OH, LOOK, DEAR!... A HARBINGER OF...

...SPRING."

"WAIT 'TILL YOU SEE HARRY'S COSTUME FOR THE PARTY!...HARRY?"

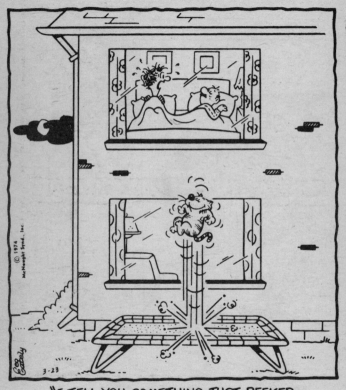

"I TELL YOU SOMETHING JUST PEEKED
IN THAT WINDOW!!"

"WE'LL USE HEATHCLIFF'S BLANKET AS A TABLECLOTH."

"CROSS OFF ANOTHER PROSPECTIVE CUSTOMER."

"WHAT COULD I DO ?... HE'S GOT THE FIVE BUCKS!"

"WHO IS THIS 'HEATHCLIFF' YOU KEEP REFERRING
TO AS THE MAJOR CAUSE OF YOUR PROFIT LOSS?"

"I GUESS HE NEVER SAW A DACHSHUND BEFORE."

"NOW, LET'S PUT IT ON THE WINDOW-SILL TO COOL."

"DID YOU PUT HEATHCLIFF OUT FOR THE NIGHT?"

"COOKIE?"

"ABOUT THIS NEW BRAND OF CAT FOOD
YOU BOYS CAME UP WITH..."

"IT'S THE ONLY WAY I CAN GET HEATHCLIFF TO TAKE HIS VITAMINS."

"I CAN'T PRACTICE WITH YOU SINGING!"

"I THINK HE'S CHECKING YOUR CREDENTIALS."

"NEVER WEAR THAT HAT AROUND HEATHCLIFF!"

"I'LL WATCH MY *OWN* WEIGHT, THANK YOU!"

"MRS. NUTMEG, I WAS WONDERING IF YOU
COULD MIND MONTAGUE FOR THE WEEKEND?"

"HE'S HAVING ONE OF THOSE DAYS."

"VISITING HOURS ARE OVER!"

"GRANDMA..."

"I WANT YOU TO GET BUSY AND CLEAN
YOUR GOLD-FISH BOWL."

"YOU'RE LUCKY IT STOPPED RAINING."

"HEATHCLIFF, I WISH YOU'D BE MORE CAREFUL
WITH YOUR RUBBER MOUSE!"

"SCAT!!"

"DO WE ACCEPT CREDIT CARDS FROM CATS?"

"WHAT DO YOU MEAN, YOU CAN'T FIND MY TEETH?!"

"ER, PROFESSOR... ABOUT YOUR EXPERIMENT
WITH THE WHITE MICE AND THE BELL..."

"HEATHCLIFF!"

"LOOK! I CAN HANDLE THIS!!"

"WATCH THIS, FRED... HEATHCLIFF CAN OPEN OUR NEW DOOR ALL BY HIMSELF!"

"HE THINKS IT'S A SCRATCHING POST."